PAUL ROMANUK

HOCKEY SUPERSTARS

2019-2020

Your complete guide to the 2019–2020 season,
featuring action photos of
your favorite players

SCHOLASTIC

TORONTO NEW YORK LONDON AUCKLAND SYDNEY
MEXICO CITY NEW DELHI HONG KONG BUENOS AIRES

THE TEAMS

WESTERN CONFERENCE – PACIFIC DIVISION

CALGARY FLAMES
team colors: red, gold, black and white
home arena: Scotiabank Saddledome
mascot: Harvey the Hound
Stanley Cups won: 1

. . . .

EDMONTON OILERS
team colors: white, royal blue and orange
home arena: Rogers Place
mascot: Hunter
Stanley Cups won: 5

. . . .

ANAHEIM DUCKS
team colors: black, gold, orange and white
home arena: Honda Center
mascot: Wild Wing
Stanley Cups won: 1

LOS ANGELES KINGS
team colors: white, black and silver
home arena: Staples Center
mascot: Bailey
Stanley Cups won: 2

. . . .

ARIZONA COYOTES
team colors: red, black, sand and white
home arena: Gila River Arena
mascot: Howler

VANCOUVER CANUCKS
team colors: blue, silver, green and white
home arena: Rogers Arena
mascot: Fin

. . . .

SAN JOSE SHARKS
team colors: teal, black, orange and white
home arena: SAP Center at San Jose
mascot: S.J. Sharkie

. . . .

VEGAS GOLDEN KNIGHTS
team colors: steel gray, gold, red and black
home arena: T-Mobile Arena
mascot: Chance

WESTERN CONFERENCE – CENTRAL DIVISION

CHICAGO BLACKHAWKS
nickname: Hawks
team colors: red, black and white
home arena: United Center
mascot: Tommy Hawk
Stanley Cups won: 6

. . . .

COLORADO AVALANCHE
nickname: Avs
team colors: burgundy, silver, black, blue and white
home arena: Pepsi Center
mascot: Bernie
Stanley Cups won: 2

DALLAS STARS
team colors: green, white, black and silver
home arena: American Airlines Center
mascot: Victor E. Green
Stanley Cups won: 1

. . . .

NASHVILLE PREDATORS
nickname: Preds
team colors: dark blue, white and gold
home arena: Bridgestone Arena
mascot: Gnash

MINNESOTA WILD
team colors: red, green, gold, wheat and white
home arena: Xcel Energy Center
mascot: Nordy

. . . .

WINNIPEG JETS
team colors: dark blue, blue, gray, silver, red and white
home arena: Bell MTS Place
mascot: Mick E. Moose

. . . .

ST. LOUIS BLUES
team colors: blue, gold, dark blue and white
home arena: Enterprise Center
mascot: Louie
Stanley Cups won: 1

EASTERN CONFERENCE – ATLANTIC DIVISION

TORONTO MAPLE LEAFS
nickname: Leafs
team colors: blue and white
home arena: Scotiabank Arena
mascot: Carlton the Bear
Stanley Cups won: 11

. . . .

BUFFALO SABRES
team colors: navy blue, gold, silver and white
home arena: KeyBank Center
mascot: Sabretooth

. . . .

FLORIDA PANTHERS
nickname: Cats
team colors: red, navy blue, yellow, gold and white
home arena: BB&T Center
mascots: Stanley C. Panther and Viktor E. Ratt

OTTAWA SENATORS
nickname: Sens
team colors: black, red, gold and white
home arena: Canadian Tire Centre
mascot: Spartacat

. . . .

TAMPA BAY LIGHTNING
nickname: Bolts
team colors: blue, black and white
home arena: Amalie Arena
mascot: ThunderBug
Stanley Cups won: 1

MONTREAL CANADIENS
nickname: Habs
team colors: red, blue and white
home arena: Bell Centre
mascot: Youppi
Stanley Cups won: 24

. . . .

DETROIT RED WINGS
nickname: Wings
team colors: red and white
home arena: Little Caesars Arena
mascot (unofficial): Al the Octopus
Stanley Cups won: 11

. . . .

BOSTON BRUINS
nickname: Bs
team colors: gold, black and white
home arena: TD Garden
mascot: Blades
Stanley Cups won: 6

EASTERN CONFERENCE – METROPOLITAN DIVISION

NEW YORK RANGERS
nickname: Blueshirts
team colors: blue, white and red
home arena: Madison Square Garden
Stanley Cups won: 4

. . . .

COLUMBUS BLUE JACKETS
nickname: Jackets
team colors: blue, red, silver and white
home arena: Nationwide Arena
mascot: Stinger

. . . .

WASHINGTON CAPITALS
nickname: Caps
team colors: red, navy blue and white
home arena: Capital One Arena
mascot: Slapshot
Stanley Cups won: 1

NEW YORK ISLANDERS
nickname: Isles
team colors: orange, blue and white
home arena: Barclays Center and Nassau Coliseum
mascot: Sparky the Dragon
Stanley Cups won: 4

. . . .

PITTSBURGH PENGUINS
nickname: Pens
team colors: black, gold and white
home arena: PPG Paints Arena
mascot: Iceburgh
Stanley Cups won: 5

PHILADELPHIA FLYERS
team colors: orange, white and black
home arena: Wells Fargo Center
mascot: Gritty
Stanley Cups won: 2

. . . .

NEW JERSEY DEVILS
team colors: red, black and white
home arena: Prudential Center
mascot: N.J. Devil
Stanley Cups won: 3

. . . .

CAROLINA HURRICANES
nickname: Canes
team colors: red, black, gray and white
home arena: PNC Arena
mascot: Stormy
Stanley Cups won: 1

YOUR FAVORITE TEAM

Name of your favorite team: _____

Conference and division: _____

Players on your favorite team at the start of the season:

Number	Name	Position
_____	_____	_____
_____	_____	_____
_____	_____	_____
_____	_____	_____
_____	_____	_____
_____	_____	_____
_____	_____	_____
_____	_____	_____
_____	_____	_____
_____	_____	_____
_____	_____	_____
_____	_____	_____
_____	_____	_____

Changes, Trades, New Players

_____ _____ _____
_____ _____ _____
_____ _____ _____
_____ _____ _____
_____ _____ _____
_____ _____ _____
_____ _____ _____

End-of-Season Standings

Fill in the name of the team you think will finish in first place in each of the four NHL divisions.

WESTERN CONFERENCE

_____ **PACIFIC DIVISION**

_____ **CENTRAL DIVISION**

EASTERN CONFERENCE

ATLANTIC DIVISION _____

METROPOLITAN DIVISION _____

The Playoffs

Which two teams will meet in the Stanley Cup Final? Fill in their names below, then circle the team you think will win.

Eastern Conference Winner: _____

Western Conference Winner: _____

YOUR FAVORITE TEAM

Your Team — All Season Long

The standings of hockey teams are listed at NHL.com and on the sports pages of the newspaper all season long. The standings will show you which team is in first place, second place, etc., right down to last place.

Some of the abbreviations you'll become familiar with are: GP for games played; W for wins; L for losses; OT for overtime losses; PTS for points; A for assists; G for goals.

Check the standings on the same day of every month and copy down what they say about your team. By keeping track of your team this way you'll be able to see when it was playing well and when it wasn't.

	GP	W	L	OT	PTS
NOVEMBER 1					
DECEMBER 1					
JANUARY 1					
FEBRUARY 1					
MARCH 1					
APRIL 1					
MAY 1					

Final Standings

At the end of the season print the final record of your team below.

YOUR TEAM	GP	W	L	OT	PTS

Your Favorite Players' Scoring Records

While you're keeping track of your favorite team during the season, you can also follow the progress of your favorite players. Just fill in their point totals on the same day of every month.

player		nov 1	dec 1	jan 1	feb 1	mar 1	apr 1	may 1

Your Favorite Goaltenders' Records

You can keep track of your favorite goaltenders' averages during the season. Just fill in the information below.

GAA is the abbreviation for goals-against average. That's the average number of goals given up by a goaltender during a game over the course of the season.

goaltender		nov 1	dec 1	jan 1	feb 1	mar 1	apr 1	may 1

BRENT BURNS

SAN JOSE SHARKS

There are many things to admire about Brent Burns's game, but one that jumps out is how well he shoots the puck. Not necessarily how *hard* he shoots (although he does have a quick, hard shot), but his ability to get shots on, or towards, the net no matter the situation.

> "It's funny. You play 1000 games. I look back, and I see just how different of a player I was. I was drafted as a winger, and I wouldn't even say a goal scoring winger. Now I go into games feeling elite and wanting to make a difference every night."

"When it comes to shooting the puck, he's one of, if not the, best I've ever seen," says San Jose coach Peter DeBoer, who has coached over 800 games in the NHL. "He has the ability to shoot the puck when he's off-balance, when the puck won't sit, when he's under pressure and from weird angles. And he gets it on net and with velocity."

Brent took more shots than any other defenseman in the league last season and led all NHL defensemen in scoring for the second time in his career. He established career highs for assists and points and finished second in balloting for the Norris Trophy as the NHL's top defenseman.

Brent also played in the 1000th game of his NHL career. It was extra special because his son, Jagger, was able to spend part of the night with his dad. Jagger had his own number 88 Sharks sweater to wear, just like Brent's. They both skated out for the pre-game ceremony through the big shark head that lowers onto the ice.

"That's one of the best moments of my life and his life," said Brent. "To share those things with him and the rest of the family, those are things you'll never forget."

The season came to a tough end for Brent as the Sharks fell to the St. Louis Blues in six games in the Western Conference Final.

"We never gave up," said Brent later. "We always sort of battled through. You always kind of thought that that magic was there. There was never doubt . . . It was always there."

The Sharks will be looking for a little more of that magic this season. They'll need it, as the Western Conference is shaping up to be another tough battle.

DID YOU KNOW?

Brent loves animals: from dogs and cats, to exotic spiders and snakes, to deer and wildebeest. When he's not playing hockey, you'll find Brent and his family with some of their exotic pets at their off-season home — a 420-acre ranch in Texas.

HOCKEY MEMORIES

Brent can remember his dad sometimes taking him to hockey practices and games on a motorcycle. "I'd be strapped on the back with my two sticks to keep me in the seat, with my hockey bag on my lap."

2018–2019 STATS

GP	G	A	PTS
82	16	67	83

Minnesota Wild's 1st choice, 20th overall, in 2003 NHL Entry Draft
1st NHL Team, Season: Minnesota Wild, 2003–2004
Born: March 9, 1985 in Barrie, Ontario
Position: Defense
Shoots: Right
Height: 1.95 m (6'5")
Weight: 104.5 kg (230 lbs.)

SIDNEY CROSBY

PITTSBURGH PENGUINS

You know a player is truly great when some of his biggest admirers are other great players. Case in point: Sidney Crosby. No one will ever mistake the NHL All-Star Game for a competitive contest. Still, it's an enjoyable event for the players. It's a chance for them to be fans for a few days, and there is no player who receives more attention from other players than Sid.

> "When I was a kid, I had posters of him all over my room. He's one of the greatest players to ever play. Just to even be around him was really cool. It was just super surreal."
> — Buffalo superstar Jack Eichel on hanging out with Sidney at the All-Star Game

"It's pretty awesome just to see him sitting in the same room across from you," said Ottawa defenseman and All-Star teammate Thomas Chabot. "It's Sid. You grew up watching him. To spend the day around him, and get to shake his hand, is pretty great."

Aside from being one of the greatest players in the history of the game, Sid has also grown into a great representative for both the sport and the NHL, and he takes his role very seriously. Sid had been battling a flu bug heading into the All-Star break. He made the trip to San Jose but had to skip Friday night's Skills Competition, and still wasn't feeling his best when he headed to the rink on Saturday. What followed was another show-stopping performance from a guy who has had many during his career. Sid lit it up with four goals and four assists and won his first-ever All-Star Game MVP Award.

"You play in it, you watch it as a kid growing up, you see the presentation, and it's pretty cool," said Sid about being presented with the award. "I had a lot of fun out there. This morning I wasn't sure how I was going to feel, but I felt a lot better than expected."

Sid played most of the games in the mini three-on-three tournament on a line with the New York Islanders' Mathew Barzal.

"I was literally laughing on the ice because it was almost too easy," said Barzal. "He was just always open. You just had to hand it off to him if you were in trouble."

Add another name to the list of Crosby admirers.

DID YOU KNOW?
Sid is one of only six players to have won the Hart Trophy as NHL MVP, the Conn Smythe as playoff MVP and the NHL All-Star Game MVP Award. The others are Jean Beliveau, Bobby Orr, Wayne Gretzky, Mario Lemieux and Joe Sakic.

HOCKEY MEMORIES
Sid gave a hockey memory to a heckler in New York that the fan will never forget. After listening to the heckler's good-natured barbs during a game last season, Sid had a signed stick delivered to him after the game! On it he wrote: "Good chirps. Take it easy on me next time!"

GP	G	A	PTS
79	35	65	100

Pittsburgh Penguins' 1st choice, 1st overall, in 2005 NHL Entry Draft
1st NHL Team, Season: Pittsburgh Penguins, 2005–2006
Born: August 7, 1987, in Cole Harbour, Nova Scotia
Position: Center
Shoots: Left
Height: 1.80 m (5'11")
Weight: 91 kg (200 lbs.)

MAX DOMI

There are trades all the time in the NHL, and most are pretty unremarkable. But some trades are packed with storylines. The one between the Arizona Coyotes and the Montreal Canadiens on June 15, 2018, had hockey fans in both cities talking. Montreal sent popular forward Alex Galchenyuk to the Arizona Coyotes in return for Max Domi. Before a puck had even hit the ice, some Montreal fans were talking about what a bad deal it was for their team. Such is life in a city with some of the most passionate and opinionated fans in sports. One thing that made this trade a little unusual is that Max is the son of Tie Domi, who played for the Toronto Maple Leafs — one of Montreal's great traditional rivals — in the 1990s and early 2000s. To say that Max grew up in a house where the Canadiens weren't exactly loved would be an understatement. He chuckled when he was asked about his dad's reaction to the trade.

"I'm his son and I'm playing for one of the most historic franchises in all of sports and he's the biggest Habs fan in the world right now," said Max. "I'm super excited to be part of it and he's just as pumped."

Max was one of the top players on the Canadiens in 2018–2019 with the best season of his young career. He led Montreal in scoring as he set career highs in goals, assists and points. Max has always taken pride in his play-making ability, so maybe his high assist total wasn't that big a surprise. But his goal total was unexpected. One reason for it? He shot the puck more than ever before.

"No words can describe the feeling of putting on that jersey for the first time. Honored to wear the crest that represents decades of history and tradition. Nos bras meurtris vous tendent le flambeau."

"I told him I'd like him to think 'shot first' sometimes before looking to pass," said Montreal coach Claude Julien. "He's really bought into that and I think it's been paying off."

For Max's part, he's been trying not to overthink things. Since the trade he's embraced the great hockey atmosphere and tradition in Montreal. A trade some Montreal fans had doubts about has turned out to be one of the team's best in recent memory.

DID YOU KNOW?

Max was diagnosed with Type I diabetes when he was 12. One of the first thngs he asked was "Can I still play hockey?" When the answer was "yes," his mindset became "we'll take care of everything in stride and just find a way to do it."

HOCKEY MEMORIES

Max couldn't get enough hockey when he was a kid. He remembers that "anyone who walked through the front door of our house was coming down to the basement to shoot some tennis balls."

2018–2019 STATS

GP	G	A	PTS
82	28	44	72

Phoenix Coyotes' 1st choice, 12th overall, in 2013 NHL Entry Draft
1st NHL Team, Season: Arizona Coyotes, 2015–2016
Born: March 2, 1995, in Winnipeg, Manitoba
Position: Center
Shoots: Left
Height: 1.78 m (5'10")
Weight: 87.5 kg (193 lbs.)

MARC-ANDRÉ FLEURY

VEGAS GOLDEN KNIGHTS

On June 15, 2017, goaltender Marc-André Fleury was standing in front of his stall in the Pittsburgh Penguins' dressing room, trying to hold back the tears as he spoke about his time with the only NHL team he had ever played for. He'd been part of three Stanley Cup titles with the Pens, the most recent just four days earlier. The NHL expansion draft was coming up in a few days; the Penguins weren't going to protect him, and he would most certainly be chosen by the expansion Vegas Golden Knights. Marc-André knew that it was the last time he would be standing in the Penguins' dressing room. What he couldn't have guessed was that one year later he'd be coming off another trip to the Stanley Cup Final, this time with Vegas. Now he is heading into year three with the Golden Knights, and still regarded as one of the best goalies in the world.

"It's weird to think back to my last year in Pittsburgh," recalls Marc-André. "I was told I was getting too old to play. Now Vegas has given me this opportunity to do what I love. I wouldn't want to go anywhere else, and hopefully I can finish my career here."

> "I'm not out here to prove anything, I just want to win games. If I can help the team get wins, that's all that matters. If I win, and the team wins, everybody's happy. At the end of the day, that's why you play."

At this point, it's a pretty safe bet that Marc-André will do just that. Now in his thirties, he is showing no sign of losing anything from his game. Last season he started 61 of the Golden Knights' 82 games and finished tied for fifth in the NHL with 35 wins. Part of the reason he has continued to play so well is that, even in the most pressure-filled situations, he tries to have fun and enjoy what he's doing.

"I've found that, for the most part, I play my best when I'm relaxed, loose and having fun," says Marc-André. "I love the game, I love to play. We have a great bunch of guys. You just have to go with the flow and have fun on the ice."

That's been the formula for Vegas: an entertaining team that has fun in front of some of the loudest fans in sports. And Marc-André is right there in the middle of it all.

DID YOU KNOW?
As well as the three Stanley Cup rings he collected in Pittsburgh, Marc-Andre left the Penguins as their all-time goaltending leader in games played (691), wins (375), shutouts (44), playoff games played (115), playoff wins (62) and playoff shut-outs (10).

HOCKEY MEMORIES
You'd think that the three Cups he's won would be on the top of Marc-Andre's list of hockey memories. They are, but right up there is his first NHL game on October 10, 2003. "That was the dream, to play in the NHL, so that first game meant a lot."

2018–2019 STATS

GP	W	L	OT	GAA	SO
61	35	21	5	2.51	8

Pittsburgh Penguins' 1st choice, 1st overall, in 2003 NHL Entry Draft
1st NHL Team, Season: Pittsburgh Penguins, 2005–2006
Born: November 28, 1984 in Sorel, Quebec
Position: Goaltender
Catches: Left
Height: 1.88 m (6'2")
Weight: 82 kg (180 lbs.)

MARK GIORDANO

CALGARY FLAMES

Mark Giordano's career is a study in the value of persistence and believing in yourself. He walked into training camp with the Ontario Hockey League's Owen Sound Attack as an undrafted and unsigned player. He left a spot in the lineup of the Calgary Flames to play in Russia for a season. And last season he finally received widespread recognition for what he has become: one of the best defensemen in the game.

> **"The risky things I've done in my career, I've always believed they would work out if you worked hard and played well enough."**

"He plays against the top people every night," says Flames general manager Brad Treliving. "He plays on every special team, he's the first guy over the boards for almost every situation in the game. He's also our leader and the conscience of our team."

Of the many great things about Mark's game, perhaps the most impressive is his consistency. Mark has managed to defy the odds as he's gotten older. At age 36, he hasn't lost a step or seen his skills erode with age — if anything, he's become even better. Last season was the finest of his 12-season NHL career, and he became only the fifth defenseman in NHL history to reach the 60-point mark at age 35 or older. He also became the first Calgary Flames defenseman ever to win the Norris Trophy.

"I take a lot of pride in working out off the ice, keeping myself in good shape," Mark said. "But still, it's not easy to play late into your 30s. We're all aware of that as players, trying to last as long as you can. To be recognized at my age with this award is a moment that's really special for me and my family."

That great work ethic helps Mark to dominate even though he's not the biggest player or the fastest player or the player with the hardest shot.

"He is a high-end player and a special character," says Calgary coach Bill Peters. "He will battle in there, battle for pucks. He's such a complete player and a guy our young guys should watch and learn from because he is special in the way he goes about his business. He's a great pro."

DID YOU KNOW?

Mark won the 2017 ESPN Muhammad Ali Sports Humanitarian Award for his work on the Team Giordano program that, among other things, assists high-needs students, encouraging positive behaviors that help lead to success in life.

HOCKEY MEMORIES

Outside of his terrific accomplishments in the NHL, Mark points to playing on Canada's Spengler Cup–winning team in 2007 as a career highlight. As he told an interviewer on the ice at the time: "This has been one of the best experiences of my career."

2018–2019 STATS

GP	G	A	PTS
78	17	57	74

Signed as a free agent by the Calgary Flames, July 6, 2004
1st NHL Team, Season: Calgary Flames, 2005–2006
Born: October 3, 1983 in Toronto, Ontario
Position: Defense
Shoots: Left
Height: 1.85 m (6'1")
Weight: 91 kg (200 lbs.)

SAN JOSE SHARKS

Success didn't come easily to Martin Jones. After being passed up in his NHL draft year, he was eventually invited to the L.A. Kings' training camp in 2008.

"It was disappointing when I didn't get drafted, but at the same time it was good motivation to work hard," said Martin. "I did have a couple of invitations to go to NHL camps and it [not getting drafted] gave me good motivation to work hard and prove people wrong."

"I push myself harder than anyone is going to push me from the outside. My motivation is to be the top goaltender in this league."

The Kings were impressed enough to sign him to an entry-level deal before returning him to his junior team, the Calgary Hitmen of the Western Hockey League. He was focused and motivated, and it showed. In his third season there, he led the WHL with an incredible 45-5-4 record. The next season he was named top goaltender in the league and helped lead the Hitmen to the WHL championship. He went on to play in the Memorial Cup and although Calgary didn't win the title, he was named the best goaltender at the tournament.

Martin turned pro with the L.A. Kings' organization and spent three seasons playing in their minor league system. His big break finally came in December 2013 when he was called up to join the Kings. He promptly won his first eight starts, including three shut-outs! But the Kings' crease was a little crowded. Jonathan Quick was the number one goalie and he wasn't going anywhere. The Kings traded Martin to the Boston Bruins, who then traded him to the San Jose Sharks. It had taken a few seasons, but Martin had finally arrived as a number one goalie in the NHL.

"When I played with him for a couple of seasons in L.A., he was a guy that was always calm back there. He plays his position well," says Jonathan Quick.

His calm approach to the game, hard work and preparation have added up to one of the highest win totals in the NHL since 2015–2016, when he joined the Sharks. Pretty impressive numbers from a player most teams overlooked.

DID YOU KNOW?
Martin has racked up 138 regular-season wins since he joined the Sharks in 2015–2016. That's the second-highest total in the NHL over that time period, after Braden Holtby's 156.

HOCKEY MEMORIES
Martin remembers starting his goaltending career when he was 10 years old, playing in a summertime minor hockey tournament. When he was a young goalie, he loved to watch Hall of Famers Patrick Roy and Martin Brodeur.

2018–2019 STATS

GP	W	L	OT	GAA	SO
62	36	19	5	2.94	3

Signed as a free agent by the Los Angeles Kings, October 2, 2008
1st NHL Team, Season: Los Angeles Kings, 2015–2016
Born: January 10, 1990, in North Vancouver, British Columbia
Position: Goaltender
Catches: Left
Height: 1.93 m (6'4")
Weight: 86 kg (190 lbs.)

NIKITA KUCHEROV

TAMPA BAY LIGHTNING

He couldn't speak a word of English when he was being considered as a draft pick by the Tampa Bay Lightning back in 2011. But at least one Tampa scout remembers the impression Nikita Kucherov made when they spoke with him at the NHL Scouting Combine leading up to the draft.

> "You don't want to be predictable. Always try to make defensemen wonder what you are going to do next. Make them confused. Use their mistakes."

"He couldn't speak any English but he looked right at you when he spoke," recalled Tampa director of amateur scouting Al Murray. "He didn't look down at the floor and talk to the interpreter like a lot of the young guys would. He looked right at us and said that he wanted to be an NHL player."

It is that kind of focus that has taken Nikita from Moscow, the city where he grew up and learned to play hockey, to the heights of NHL stardom. Last season he was named winner of both the Hart Trophy as NHL MVP and the Ted Lindsay Award as the league's most outstanding player as selected by the players.

"It's what you have in here," says Tampa coach Jon Cooper, tapping his chest. "He's got passion and he's got heart. He has amazing ability too, but you watch so many players that have all the ability and they don't pan out because they don't have that [heart]."

Nikita has never been better than he was last season. He won his first NHL scoring title, hitting career highs in goals, assists and points as he led the Bolts in scoring for the fourth straight season. He really took off during the month of December, when he burned his way to the top of the NHL scoring race — scorching through opponents and setting a team record for most points in a calendar month. In 14 games during December Nikita had 30 points (9-21-30).

For all of the personal success Nikita attained last season, team success eluded him as the Lightning were swept in the first round of the playoffs by Columbus — giving him all the motivation he needs to be even better this season.

DID YOU KNOW?

Nikita has been known to study what makes other great goal scorers successful — like the way Alex Ovechkin gets his shot away so quickly, or how Patrick Kane creates time and space near the net to get a scoring chance.

HOCKEY MEMORIES

Nikita got into hockey when he was a young boy and his family moved to Moscow. "It was an accident. My mother went to look for a job and we were passing a hockey rink and she went in and got work and then decided to bring me along to work, to play hockey."

2018–2019 STATS

GP	G	A	PTS
82	41	87	128

Tampa Bay Lightning's 2nd choice, 58th overall, in 2011 NHL Entry Draft
1st NHL Team, Season: Tampa Bay Lightning, 2013–2014
Born: June 17, 1993, in Maykop, Russia
Position: Right Wing
Shoots: Left
Height: 1.80 m (5'11")
Weight: 81 kg (178 lbs.)

MITCH MARNER

Even if Mitch Marner is playing against your favorite team, there is probably still a little part of you that enjoys watching him play. He always looks as though he's about to break into a big grin. He weaves his way through traffic with the puck, narrowly avoiding getting crunched by an opponent, before getting away a shot on goal or feeding a linemate with a nice pass. All done with the air of someone who absolutely loves what he's doing. He has one of the all-time great positive attitudes in the game.

"There's going to be ups and downs, and it's about how you handle yourself through those ups and downs. Everything isn't always going to be sunny and beautiful. When you do hit one of those drops, it's about finding a way to get out of it as quick as possible."

"I'd tell anyone getting into this game to have fun, enjoy the time, enjoy the moments," says Mitch. "There are always going to be ups and downs and moments that you hate. That happens to every hockey player, I don't care who you are. But you should make sure you enjoy the moment."

Despite the Leafs being knocked out in the first round of the playoffs by Boston, there was much to enjoy for Mitch last season as he set career highs in goals, assists and points. He spent most of the season playing alongside veteran John Tavares, and the two seemed to complement one another.

"I was really excited about playing with him," recalls Mitch about hearing the news that Tavares had signed with the Leafs. "He was a guy that you watched when you were playing minor hockey and you looked up to. He did everything we all expected, and more."

Whether the difference was playing on a line with Tavares, or just taking the next step in his career development, Mitch really did move up to a higher level last season. And although the first-round loss was tough to swallow, Mitch is all about looking ahead to this season and taking another big step forward.

"I think, as a team, we take this forward," said Mitch after the playoff defeat. "We can come back next year hungrier and know what we have to be better at."

DID YOU KNOW?

In January of 2019 Marner became the first player in Toronto Maple Leafs history to top the 60-point mark in each of his first three seasons. Auston Matthews followed suit a few weeks later.

HOCKEY MEMORIES

Mitch was on the ice for the first time at the age of two. He fell a lot. But by the next day, he was pushing a puck around the ice with a sawed-off hockey stick.

2018–2019 STATS

GP	G	A	PTS
82	26	68	94

Toronto Maple Leafs' 1st choice, 4th overall, in 2015 NHL Entry Draft
1st NHL Team, Season: Toronto Maple Leafs, 2016–2017
Born: May 5, 1997 in Markham, Ontario
Position: Right Wing
Shoots: Right
Height: 1.83 m (6'0")
Weight: 79.5 kg (175 lbs.)

CONNOR McDAVID

Connor McDavid is the best, and most important, player on a team that is struggling to make the transition from being a team with potential to a team that can win consistently and go deep into the playoffs. You would expect him to be feeling a healthy dose of pressure under those circumstances, but he says that's not the case.

> "It's not like a switch is just going to get flicked and we're going to be a good hockey team. It's going to take a collective work ethic and guys buying in. And also a lot of hard work."

"I have never really been affected by outside pressure. I have my own internal pressures to work hard, play well, be my best. That's really all I've ever worried about," says Connor.

There was certainly more than enough pressure, felt or not, to go around in Edmonton last season. There was a coaching change in November, when Todd McLellan was replaced by Ken Hitchcock. In January, the Oilers fired general manager Peter Chiarelli. It was a season of more frustration for players and fans and hardly a surprise that the team finished out of the playoff picture for the 12th time in the last 13 seasons.

At the All-Star Game media day a reporter asked Connor whether he was frustrated enough that he "wanted out of Edmonton." Connor just shook his head.

"That's just not the case at all. I'm here to be part of the solution. That's all I'm going to say on that."

On a personal level, it was another outstanding season for Connor. In fact, he recorded the highest points total of his career, topping the 100-point mark for the third consecutive season, finishing second in the scoring and leading the Oilers with 116 points. However, once again the Oilers as a team were not able to match the success of their superstar player.

"We hear the boos [from the fans] and hear all the stuff that's going on," said Connor after a tough game last January. "We understand that the fans are frustrated. We expect more from ourselves and the fans obviously expect better of us. We need to be better."

DID YOU KNOW?
Connor has won the All-Star Skills Competition fastest skater race three years in a row. There were rumors last year that other players didn't want to participate because none of them believed they could beat him!

HOCKEY MEMORIES
Connor still remembers receiving a brand new Easton Synergy hockey stick from Santa the Christmas he was eight. He could hardly wait to use it in a game. Connor had to wait a couple of days until his team played in a tournament but he put it to good use, picking up five points in his first game.

2018–2019 STATS

GP	G	A	PTS
78	41	75	116

Edmonton Oilers' 1st choice, 1st overall, in 2015 NHL Entry Draft
1st NHL Team, Season: Edmonton Oilers, 2015–2016
Born: January 13, 1997, in Richmond Hill, Ontario
Position: Center
Shoots: Left
Height: 1.85 m (6'1")
Weight: 87.5 kg (193 lbs.)

ALEX OVECHKIN

A question you often hear asked of NHL players who have been fortunate enough to win a Stanley Cup Championship is "What's next? How do you top that?" And the standard answer, including from Alex Ovechkin? "You do it again!"

"Right now, it's pretty much set in stone that he's probably the greatest Capital that has ever played."
— Hockey Hall of Fame member and former Washington superstar Mike Gartner

---

"As soon as you taste it, you don't want to let it go," said Alex, heading into last season. "That moment that we all had, we will never forget. As soon as you start talking about it with your teammates, you go, 'We have to do this again. We have to repeat.'"

It was a tall order. Since 2000 only one team has won back-to-back Cups (Pittsburgh, 2016 and 2017), and the Caps were upset in the opening round last season by Carolina.

On an individual level, Alex was as good last season as he's ever been. Those who watch him every day say that if there was any change

at all, it was that he was more intense and an even better leader than the previous season. He played as a defending champion. No games, wins or points were taken for granted.

"You learn that every point, every game is going to count because that will get you to the playoffs," said Ovie. "If you don't push yourself right now, it may be too hard to push at the end."

Alex won the Maurice Richard Trophy as the NHL's leading goal scorer for the sixth time in the last seven seasons and the eighth time in his career. Since that trophy was first presented in 1999, no other player has come close to Ovie's total. He is, without a doubt, the greatest goal scorer of his era. There are better all-around players, but no one has scored goals the way Alex has. At the end of last season he led all active NHL players with 658 career goals, ranking him 13th on the all-time career goals list. It looks like Alex will crack the top 10 this season. But that isn't the stat that will be feeding his competitive fire. Ovie will be all about winning another Cup.

DID YOU KNOW?

Ovie is the highest scoring Russian player in NHL history. He passed one of his hockey heroes, Sergei Federov, during a game last February against the Vancouver Canucks. Fedorov finished his career with 1179 points.

HOCKEY MEMORIES

Taking the Cup to Moscow after he'd won it for the first time meant so much to Alex. "I took it to the hockey school where I learned to play. To bring the Cup to all those people there who helped me out when I was a little kid was something special."

2018–2019 STATS

GP	G	A	PTS
81	51	38	89

Washington Capitals' 1st choice, 1st overall, in 2004 NHL Entry Draft
1st NHL Team, Season: Washington Capitals, 2005–2006
Born: September 17, 1985, in Moscow, USSR (now Russia)
Position: Left Wing
Shoots: Right
Height: 1.90 m (6'3")
Weight: 106.5 kg (235 lbs.)

DAVID PASTRNAK

The Boston Bruins are one of the oldest franchises in the NHL. The list of great players who have worn the "B" on the front of their sweater could fill this page. And even at this early stage of his career, David Pastrnak's name would have to be on that list. In 2016–2017, at the age of 20 years and 294 days, he became the youngest Bruin ever to score 30 goals in a season.

> "You have to be good on defense too. If you want to be a good hockey player you have to play for the team, and you don't play for the team just with scoring."

David was drafted by the Bruins in the first round of the 2014 NHL Entry Draft. NHL teams will usually meet before the draft with some of the top players they are thinking about selecting. To David, those meetings made him feel like Boston could be the place for him.

"Right at the beginning, I felt that they were great people and there was a great meeting. I didn't have it like that with other teams," recalled David.

"You could tell as soon as you met him that he just loves to play hockey," says Bruins GM Don Sweeney. "He has a bit of flair on and off the ice and he's excited. I think it's infectious for everybody."

David has had some memorable games for someone who has only been in the league for five seasons. One of his biggest nights took place on a big stage — the opening round of the 2018 Stanley Cup playoffs. It was game two of the Bruins' series against the Toronto Maple Leafs and David and his linemates, Brad Marchand and Patrice Bergeron, were on fire! David had a hat trick and three assists, breaking Wayne Gretzky's 1983 record to become the youngest player in NHL history to have a six-point night in the playoffs.

The Pastrnak production continued to roll last season as he put up the best numbers of his career. He led his team with 38 goals and had a career-best 81 points, including a five-point night (3 goals, 2 assists) on March 27 against the New York Rangers.

The list of accomplishments continues to grow, and David's love for the game continues to burn as brightly as ever.

DID YOU KNOW?

David moved from the Czech Republic to Sweden to play hockey when he was only 15. He spent a couple of seasons in the Swedish Hockey League with Södertälje, where he played with future Toronto Maple Leafs forward William Nylander.

HOCKEY MEMORIES

David's hero and most important hockey teacher was his dad, Milan, who passed away in 2013. Milan didn't live long enough to see his son get drafted, but David has never forgotten the advice his dad gave him: "Always practice hard and work hard."

2018–2019 STATS

GP	G	A	PTS
66	38	43	81

Boston Bruins' 1st choice, 25th overall, in 2014 NHL Entry Draft
1st NHL Team, Season: Boston Bruins, 2014–2015
Born: May 25, 1996, in Havirov, Czech Republic
Position: Right Wing
Shoots: Right
Height: 1.83 m (6'0")
Weight: 88 kg (194 lbs.)

ELIAS PETTERSSON

VANCOUVER CANUCKS

The last few seasons have been a mixed bag for theVancouver Canucks. The team hasn't played a post-season game since 2015, and after the 2017–2018 season Daniel and Henrik Sedin retired. Their departure left a big hole to fill; the Sedins had been the faces of the franchise for a generation of fans. But there has been good news too. The team is developing a solid core of young players who are poised to lead the club to future success. On the top of that list is NHL rookie of the year Elias Pettersson, whose 66 points led all NHL rookies in scoring and set a Canucks record for most points by a rookie.

> "What he's done for the fans and this city already is tremendous. He's coming into this league and getting 10 goals in his first 10 games? That's something no one really does. He's a special player."
> — Vancouver teammate Brock Boeser

Big things were expected of Elias heading into last season. He was a high first-round pick in the 2017 draft, and he followed up his draft year with a spectacular season in the Swedish Hockey League. He was part of a league championship with Växjö and was named SHL Rookie of the Year, Forward of the Year and MVP. He also won the scoring title and his 56 points set a record for the most points by a 19-year-old.

"It helped me, playing a year in that league," says Elias. "On the ice, it helped my confidence. Off the ice, I started getting used to all the attention."

Vancouver management and fans were eager to see how he would do in the NHL. They didn't have to wait long for an answer! Elias scored 13:48 into his first NHL game, beating Calgary goalie Mike Smith with a beautifully placed wrist shot from the middle of the right faceoff circle. Elias went on to score 10 goals in his first 10 games.

"I always believe in myself. But, to be honest, growing up, I didn't think I would play in the NHL," said Elias. "But I always practiced hard and was always working and taking it step-by-step. Now I'm here, living my dream. But nothing has come easy."

It may not have been easy, but like other great players, Elias can sure make it look like it was.

DID YOU KNOW?

Elias is a man of many talents. As well as being a great hockey player, he is able to juggle and has learned how to ride a unicycle. It is not yet known if he can do both at the same time.

HOCKEY MEMORIES

Elias recalls that his typical day as a kid would be to go to school, then to a local free skate for a couple of hours. After dinner he would go to the local rink, where his dad drove the Zamboni, to practice some more before bedtme.

2018–2019 STATS

GP	G	A	PTS
71	28	38	66

Vancouver Canucks' 1st choice, 5th overall, in 2017 NHL Entry Draft
1st NHL Team, Season: Vancouver Canucks, 2018–2019
Born: November 12, 1998 in Sundsvall, Sweden
Position: Center/Right Wing
Shoots: Left
Height: 1.88 m (6'2")
Weight: 80 kg (176 lbs.)

BRAYDEN POINT

TAMPA BAY LIGHTNING

Brayden Point was not on any list of top picks heading into the 2014 NHL Entry Draft. Even though he was coming off a team-leading 91-point season with the Moose Jaw Warriors in the WHL, many scouts had concerns about both his size and his skating ability. Brayden wasn't picked in the first round, or the second. The Tampa Bay Lightning plucked him in the third round, and what a steal that has turned out to be! Last season, his third in the NHL, Brayden tied with Nikita Kucherov for second on the team in goals. Of the 76 players from the 2014 draft year who have played in the NHL, Brayden is fourth in goal scoring, with 91. And of the seven players Tampa selected in that draft, Point is by far the most successful. He's played more games and has scored more points than any of the others.

> "He has proven to myself and to everybody in that locker room that he's a top hockey player in this league."
> — Tampa Bay coach Jon Cooper

"I was really lucky to be drafted by a team that wanted me and wanted to develop my game so that I had all the tools to play in the NHL," Brayden says.

Brayden spent the next two seasons at the junior level, working hard to become a complete player with a solid, well-rounded game. Heading into his fourth NHL season, he can be on the ice in almost any situation. He works the power play, he takes important faceoffs and he often matches up against the other team's top players.

"I think one of the things about his game that maybe gets overlooked is his ability to check," says teammate Steven Stamkos. "He plays against top lines a lot and has a role trying to shut them down. He has great speed and great hockey sense. Those two things are a pretty lethal combination."

When Brayden looks around, hears and reads the things other people are saying about him, including that he's a "superstar," it can all seem a touch unreal.

"I don't really believe that I'm a star in this league," said Brayden last season.

He might be the only guy in the league who thinks that.

DID YOU KNOW?

Brayden has worked on his skating skills with former Canadian and World Champion figure skater Barbara Underhill. "She definitely helped me gain a step in the corners, and also to be on the good part of my blade in turns," he says.

HOCKEY MEMORIES

Brayden's junior hockey debut came in the 2011–2012 season, as a 15-year-old with the Canmore Eagles of the Alberta Junior Hockey League. He played on the same line as his brother Riley and assisted on Riley's game-winning goal.

GP	G	A	PTS
79	41	51	92

Tampa Bay Lightning's 4th choice, 79th overall, in 2014 NHL Entry Draft
1st NHL Team: Tampa Bay Lightning, 2016–2017
Born: March 13, 1996, in Calgary, Alberta
Position: Center
Shoots: Right
Height: 1.78 m (5'10")
Weight: 75.5 kg (166 lbs.)

MORGAN RIELLY

TORONTO MAPLE LEAFS

When Morgan Rielly looks back on his NHL career he will remember the 2018–2019 season as the one in which he stepped up a level to become an elite defenseman.

Morgan's previous career high for goals in a season was 9. He'd matched that total by the time he'd played 20 games last season. Morgan wound up with the best numbers of his career, leading all NHL defensemen in goals and finishing third in scoring among defensemen. His 72 points were the best season total for a Toronto defenseman since 1978–1979 when Borje Salming had 73 (the team record is held by Ian Turnbull, who had 79 points in 1976–1977).

"I think when he first got to the league he was just trying to make a name for himself. Now he's got confidence and swagger in his game."
— Toronto teammate Jake Gardiner

"People like to talk about the points. I can genuinely say that it's not something I think about," says Morgan. "When I was younger I would. But I find as I get older that I put that stuff out of my mind and just think about playing."

Last season Morgan seemed to be playing with more confidence than ever before.

"He's always had that ability to see plays develop and have that offensive awareness," said his pal Jake Gardiner, "but his confidence is great and when he sees a chance he's going to go for it."

As much as Morgan's season was about the great offensive numbers — points and goals are what grab headlines — he also made sure his defensive responsibilities didn't suffer. Since Mike Babcock took over as Toronto head coach in 2015–2016, he has worked hard with Morgan to improve that part of his game.

"We all knew about the offensive part of his game," said Babcock. "But he's really improved the defensive part of his game. That's been a huge difference. His stick and his feet in the d-zone and his defensive awareness has gotten way better."

How much better can Morgan get? Is there a Norris Trophy in his future? He has the best chance of any Toronto defenseman in many, many years.

DID YOU KNOW?

Rielly's favorite Christmas tradition is to watch the movie *National Lampoon's Christmas Vacation* with his family. "It never gets old, I still love it and it's pretty special to me," says Morgan.

HOCKEY MEMORIES

"I'll always remember being at the NHL Draft in 2012 and hearing my name called. That's pretty special. To be drafted to Toronto was an added bonus."

2018–2019 STATS

GP	G	A	PTS
82	20	52	72

Toronto Maple Leafs' 1st choice, 5th overall, in 2012 NHL Entry Draft
1st NHL Team, Season: Toronto Maple Leafs, 2013–2014
Born: March 9, 1994, in Vancouver, British Columbia
Position: Defense
Catches: Left
Height: 1.85 m (6'1")
Weight: 100 kg (221 lbs.)

PEKKA RINNE

What an amazing career Pekka Rinne has had. He learned to play the game in his native Finland, was a very late NHL draft pick and spent a few seasons battling in the minors before finally emerging as one of the best goalies of this era. He's become one of the elder statesmen of both the goaltending position and the Nashville Predators franchise.

> "He's done it for so long. At times I think he's gotten lost in the shuffle in a quieter market here in Nashville. I think as he's gotten older, he's gotten better."
> — Nashville defenseman Ryan Ellis

"To me, when I signed that long-term deal [in 2012], I felt a huge burden," recalls Pekka. "I wondered if I'm ever going to be worth it. You put a lot of everything on one player, and I wasn't quite sure whether I was ready for that."

He was, it turns out, very much ready. Pekka enters this season having started over 600 games in the NHL — every single one of them for Nashville. It is rare in this era for players to spend their entire career with one team, and it means a lot to Pekka that Nashville's has been the only sweater he's ever worn in the NHL.

"I was 22 when I came to this organization. I spent 3 years in Milwaukee and now 10 years here. Nashville is my second home. It's where I've spent my adulthood and grown up as a man and as a person. Hopefully, one day, I can end my playing days here."

How much longer can Pekka play at the level he's been playing? He still puts up solid numbers, but the Preds also have a young goalie, Juuse Saros, who probably wants to play more than he has the last couple of seasons.

"I feel like I have good years left," said Pekka last season. "At the same time I am excited for Saros, who is up-and-coming. He's ready and he's more ready every year that goes by. Maybe my job at some point is to be a mentor or something. But I still feel good and don't want to get too far ahead."

Wherever the path leads, it's hard to picture Pekka anywhere but in Nashville. That's how he wants it and that's how his teammates and fans of the Preds want it as well.

DID YOU KNOW?

Pekka loves hockey, but he also loves dogs. Late last season he adopted a Bernedoodle puppy named Pabla. He even brought the dog to practice, where he happily posed for a few pictures with his new pal.

HOCKEY MEMORIES

Playing in the 2017 Stanley Cup Final against Pittsburgh is a bittersweet memory for Pekka. The Preds lost in six games but the vibe in the city is something he'll remember. "I'll never forget the hundred thousand people, flooding the streets of downtown before game six . . . cheering for us."

2018–2019 STATS

GP	W	L	OT	GAA	SO
56	30	19	4	2.42	4

Nashville Predators' 31st choice, 258th overall, in 2004 NHL Entry Draft
1st NHL Team, Season: Nashville Predators, 2008–2009
Born: November 3, 1982, in Kempele, Finland
Position: Goaltender
Catches: Left
Height: 1.95 m (6'5")
Weight: 98.5 kg (217 lbs.)

MARK SCHEIFELE

WINNIPEG JET

Mark Scheifele is often described as a student of the game.

Mark's dedication to learning the game, then taking what he'd learned and applying it, paid off when he was drafted seventh overall by the Winnipeg Jets in 2011. Despite being a high pick and showing promise at a couple of training camps, Mark was eventually returned to his junior club for both the 2011–2012 and 2012–2013 seasons. There were some who wondered whether the Jets had blown it on their first-round pick.

"I'm what you might call a full-on hockey nerd. I can watch hockey all day. You watch any hockey game closely enough and there's going to be something you can pick up."

"I can remember back in 2012, after Scheif had been sent back to junior for the second straight season," said Winnipeg coach Paul Maurice, "and I was doing some TV work with TSN. The question that night on one of the panel discussions was: 'Is Mark Scheifele a bust?' Because the kid didn't make the NHL when he was 18 and light it up for

30 goals, people were wondering whether or not he was a bust. I'd love to know what those people think now."

It was the 2015–2016 season when Mark really started to hit his stride as a dominant NHL center, leading the team with 29 goals and finishing second in team scoring with 61 points. He's followed that up by topping the 80-point mark in two of the last three seasons, including a career-high 84 points and a team best-38 goals last season.

"I've always been a guy who wants to get better every summer," says Mark. "If I can make myself 10 percent better, then I've just made the team 10 percent better. You can never stop working."

That's Mark: working hard and always striving to improve. With that kind of determination and work ethic, he's not only a student of the game but also a pretty good teacher.

DID YOU KNOW?
Mark started wearing the number 55 when he was playing minor hockey in his hometown of Kitchener, Ontario, because that's the number his older brother used to wear.

HOCKEY MEMORIES
Many of Mark's early memories of the sport are of Rollerblade hockey, not hockey on ice. His mom, Mary Lou, recalls that "in the summertime he'd live in his Rollerblades. Play all day, keep them on for dinner, and head back out after."

2018–2019 STATS

GP	G	A	PTS
82	38	46	84

Winnipeg Jets' 1st choice, 7th overall, in 2011 NHL Entry Draft
1st NHL Team, Season: Winnipeg Jets, 2011–2012
Born: March 15, 1993, in Kitchener, Ontario
Position: Center
Shoots: Right
Height: 1.90 m (6'3")
Weight: 94 kg (207 lbs.)

REFEREE SIGNALS

Do you know what is happening when the referee stops play and makes a penalty call? If you don't, then you're missing an important part of the game. The referee can call different penalties that result in anything from playing a man short for two minutes to having a player kicked out of the game.

Here are some of the most common referee signals. Now you'll know what penalties are being called against your team.

Boarding
Checking an opponent into the boards in a violent way.

Charging
Checking an opponent in a violent way as a result of skating or charging at him.

Cross-checking
Striking an opponent with the stick, while both hands are on the stick and both arms are extended.

Elbowing
Checking an opponent with an elbow.

High-sticking
Striking an opponent with the stick, which is held above shoulder height.

Holding
Holding back an opponent with the hands or arms.

Hooking
Using the blade of the stick to hold back an opponent.

Icing
Shooting the puck across the opposing team's goal line from one's own side of the rink. Called only if the opposing player touches the puck first.

Interference
Holding back an opponent who does not have the puck in play.

Kneeing
Using a knee to hold back an opponent.

Misconduct
A ten-minute penalty – the longest type called. Usually for abuse of an official.

Roughing
Shoving or striking an opponent.

REFEREE SIGNALS

Slashing
Using the stick to strike an opponent.

Spearing
Poking an opponent with the blade of the stick.

Slow whistle
The official waits to blow his whistle because of a delayed offside or delayed penalty call. Done while the opposing team has control of the puck.

Tripping
Tripping an opponent with the stick, a hand or a foot.

Unsportsmanlike conduct
Showing poor sportsmanship toward an opponent. For example: biting, pulling hair, etc.

Wash-out
Goal not allowed.

FINAL TEAM STANDINGS 2018-2019

EASTERN CONFERENCE

Atlantic Division

Team	GP	W	L	OT	PTS
TAMPA BAY	82	62	16	4	128
BOSTON	82	49	24	9	107
TORONTO	82	46	28	8	100
MONTREAL	82	44	30	8	96
FLORIDA	82	36	32	14	86
BUFFALO	82	33	39	10	76
DETROIT	82	32	40	10	74
OTTAWA	82	29	47	6	64

Metropolitan Division

Team	GP	W	L	OT	PTS
WASHINGTON	82	48	26	8	104
NY ISLANDERS	82	48	27	7	103
PITTSBURGH	82	44	26	12	100
CAROLINA	82	46	29	7	99
COLUMBUS	82	47	31	4	98
PHILADELPHIA	82	37	37	8	82
NY RANGERS	82	32	36	14	78
NEW JERSEY	82	31	41	10	72

WESTERN CONFERENCE

Pacific Division

Team	GP	W	L	OT	PTS
CALGARY	82	50	25	7	107
SAN JOSE	82	46	27	9	101
VEGAS	82	43	32	7	93
ARIZONA	82	39	35	8	86
VANCOUVER	82	35	36	11	81
ANAHEIM	82	35	37	10	80
EDMONTON	82	35	38	9	79
LOS ANGELES	82	31	42	9	71

Central Division

Team	GP	W	L	OT	PTS
NASHVILLE	82	47	29	6	100
WINNIPEG	82	47	30	5	99
ST. LOUIS	82	45	28	9	99
DALLAS	82	43	32	7	93
COLORADO	82	38	30	14	90
CHICAGO	82	36	34	12	84
MINNESOTA	82	37	36	9	83

GP = Games played; W = Wins; L = Losses; OT = Overtime losses; PTS = Points

Top Ten Points Leaders 2018-2019

	PLAYER	TEAM	GP	G	A	P	S	S%
1	NIKITA KUCHEROV	TAMPA BAY	82	41	87	128	246	16.7
2	CONNOR McDAVID	EDMONTON	78	41	75	116	240	17.1
3	PATRICK KANE	CHICAGO	81	44	66	110	341	12.9
4	LEON DRAISAITL	EDMONTON	82	50	55	105	231	21.6
5	BRAD MARCHAND	BOSTON	79	36	64	100	231	15.6
6	SIDNEY CROSBY	PITTSBURGH	79	35	65	100	220	15.9
7	NATHAN MacKINNON	COLORADO	82	41	58	99	365	11.2
8	JOHNNY GAUDREAU	CALGARY	82	36	63	99	245	14.7
9	STEVEN STAMKOS	TAMPA BAY	82	45	53	98	234	19.2
10	ALEKSANDER BARKOV	FLORIDA	82	35	61	96	206	17.0

GP = Games played; G = Goals; A = Assists; P = Points;
S = Shots; S% = Percentage

Top Ten Goalies — Total Wins 2018-2019

	PLAYER	TEAM	GP	W	L	OT	SA%	GA	GAA
1	ANDREI VASILEVSKIY	TAMPA BAY	53	39	10	4	.925	128	2.40
2	SERGEI BOBROVSKY	COLUMBUS	62	37	24	1	.913	153	2.58
3	FREDERIK ANDERSEN	TORONTO	60	36	16	7	.917	162	2.77
4	MARTIN JONES	SAN JOSE	62	36	19	5	.896	176	2.94
5	CAREY PRICE	MONTREAL	66	35	24	6	.918	161	2.49
6	MARC-ANDRE FLEURY	VEGAS	61	35	21	5	.913	152	2.51
7	CONNOR HELLEBUYCK	WINNIPEG	63	34	23	3	.913	179	2.90
8	BRADEN HOLTBY	WASHINGTON	59	32	19	5	.911	160	2.82
9	DEVAN DUBNYK	MINNESOTA	67	31	28	6	.913	163	2.54
10	PEKKA RINNE	NASHVILLE	56	30	19	4	.918	130	2.42

GP = Games played; W = Wins; L = Losses; OT = Overtime and/or Shut-Out Losses;
SA% = Save percentage; GA = Goals Against; GAA = Goals-Against Average

END-OF-SEASON STATS

Countdown to the Cup 2019–2020

EASTERN CONFERENCE

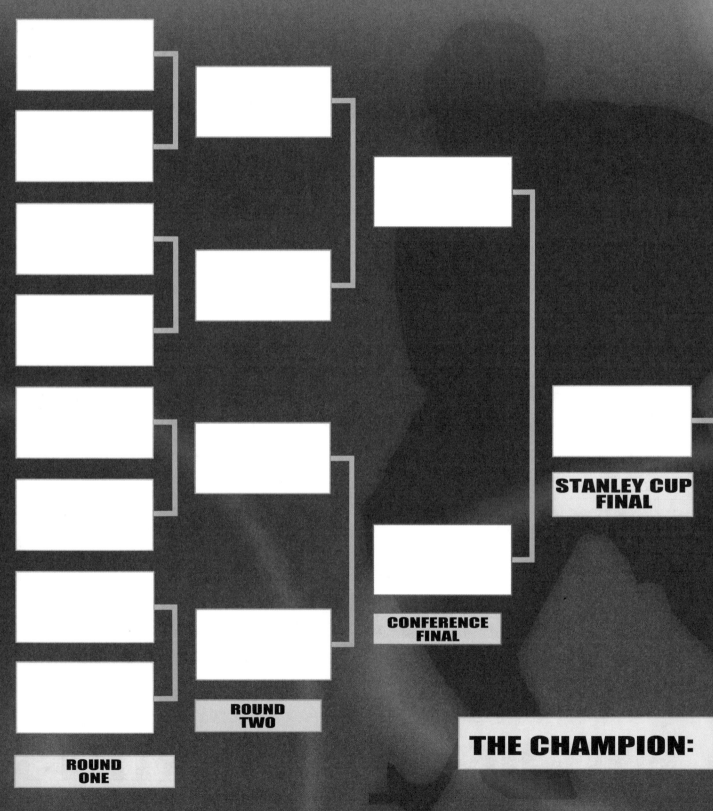

STANLEY CUP
FINAL

CONFERENCE
FINAL

ROUND
TWO

ROUND
ONE

THE CHAMPION:

WESTERN CONFERENCE

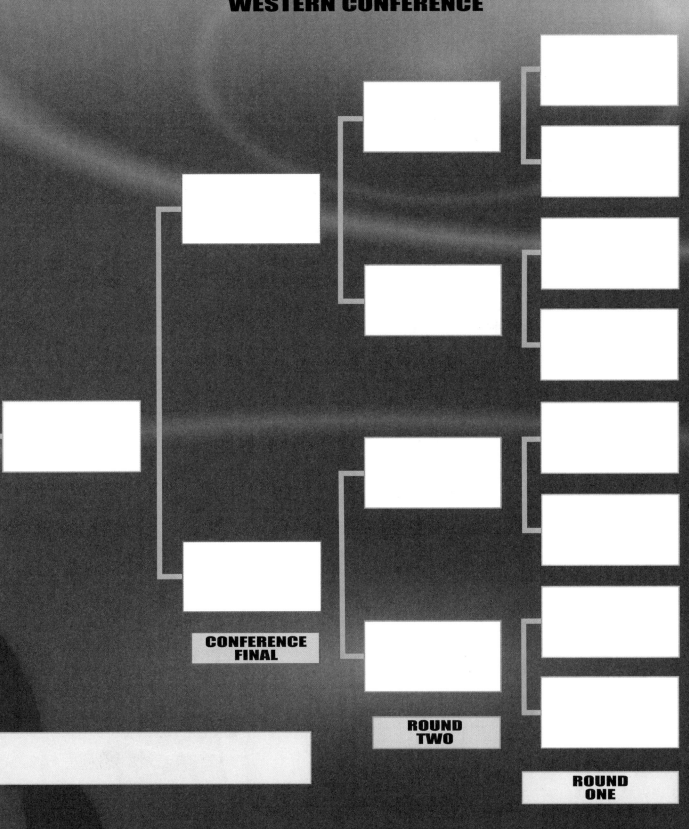

CONFERENCE
FINAL

ROUND
TWO

ROUND
ONE

NHL AWARDS

Here are some of the major NHL awards for individual players. Fill in your selection for each award and then fill in the name of the actual winner of the trophy.

HART MEMORIAL TROPHY

Awarded to the player judged to be the most valuable to his team. Selected by the Professional Hockey Writers Association.

2019 winner: **Nikita Kucherov**

Your choice for 2020: _____

The winner: _____

ART ROSS TROPHY

Awarded to the player who leads the league in scoring points at the end of the regular season.

2019 winner: **Nikita Kucherov**

Your choice for 2020: _____

The winner: _____

CALDER MEMORIAL TROPHY

Awarded to the player selected as the most proficient in his first year of competition in the NHL. Selected by the Professional Hockey Writers Association.

2019 winner: **Elias Pettersson**

Your choice for 2020: _____

The winner: _____

JAMES NORRIS TROPHY

Awarded to the defense player who demonstrates throughout his season the greatest all-round ability. Selected by the Professional Hockey Writers Association.

2019 winner: **Mark Giordano**

Your choice for 2020: _____

The winner: _____

VEZINA TROPHY

Awarded to the goalkeeper judged to be the best. Selected by the NHL general managers.

2019 winner: **Andrei Vasilevskiy**

Your choice for 2020: _____

The winner: _____

MAURICE RICHARD TROPHY

Awarded to the player who scores the highest number of regular-season goals.

2019 winner: **Alex Ovechkin**

Your choice for 2020: _____

The winner: _____

WILLIAM M. JENNINGS TROPHY

Awarded to the goalkeeper(s) who played a minimum of 25 games for the team with the fewest goals scored against it.

2019 winner: **Robin Lehner/ Thomas Greiss**

Your choice for 2020: _____

The winner: _____

LADY BYNG MEMORIAL TROPHY

Awarded to the player judged to have exhibited the best sportsmanship combined with a high standard of playing ability. Selected by the Professional Hockey Writers Association.

2019 winner: **Aleksander Barkov**

Your choice for 2020: _____

The winner: _____

FRANK J. SELKE TROPHY

Awarded to the forward who best excels in the defensive aspects of the game. Selected by the Professional Hockey Writers Association.

2019 winner: **Ryan O'Reilly**

Your choice for 2020: _____

The winner: _____

CONN SMYTHE TROPHY

Awarded to the player most valuable to his team in the Stanley Cup playoffs. Selected by the Professional Hockey Writers Association.

2019 winner: **Ryan O'Reilly**

Your choice for 2020: _____

The winner: _____

BILL MASTERTON MEMORIAL TROPHY

Awarded to the player who best exemplifies the qualitites of perseverance, sportsmanship and dedication to hockey. Selected by the Professional Hockey Writers Association.

2019 winner: **Robin Lehner**

Your choice for 2020: _____

The winner: _____

FUTURE STARS?

Drafting players for NHL teams is a tough job. For example, of the 211 players taken in the 2009 NHL Entry Draft, only 62 (29.4%) have suited up for 120 or games more in the NHL. Ninety-four of the players drafted (44.5%) didn't play a single NHL game. It can be a bit of a guessing game, but here are some players we think will make the grade and have long careers.

Jack Hughes

Kirby Dach

Bowen Byram

JACK HUGHES
Center
1.78 m (5'10") / 77.5 kg (171 lbs.)
Born: May 14, 2001, in Orlando, Florida
Drafted: 1st by New Jersey Devils
2018–2019 Club: U.S. National Team
Development Program

KIRBY DACH
Center
1.93 m (6'4") / 90 kg (198 lbs.)
Born: January 21, 2001, in St. Albert, Alberta
Drafted: 3rd by Chicago Blackhawks
2018–2019 Club: Saskatoon Blades, WHL

BOWEN BYRAM
Defense
1.85 m (6'1") / 88.5 kg (195 lbs.)
Born: June 13, 2001, in Cranbrook,
British Columbia
Drafted: 4th by Colorado Avalanche
2018–2019 Club: Vancouver Giants, WHL

KAAPO KAKKO
Right Wing
1.88 m (6'2") / 88 kg (194 lbs.)
Born: February 13, 2001, in Turku, Finland
Drafted: 2nd by New York Rangers
2018–2019 Club: TPS Turku, Finnish Liiga